THOSE
SPIKES OF
SPIKE
MILLIGAN

THOSE SPIKES OF SPIKE MILLIGAN

The Distinct Life and Humor of Spike Milligan, in Short

Author: Natasha Tristan

Dedication

Dedicated to Almighty.

DISCLAIMER

The information provided in this book is best prepared from our knowledge and methods of findings. We have made every effort to ensure the accuracy and reliability of the details given in this. Anyhow, the information is included "as is" without any warranty of any kind. We do not assume any responsibility or obligation for the accuracy, content, completeness, legitimacy, and reliability of the information consisted in this book.

Acknowledgments

Greatly thankful to everyone for their immense support for the release of this book.

CONTENTS

SPIKE MILLIGAN, A COMEDY GENIUS

Spike Milligan's real name is Terence Alan Sean Milligan. He was born on April 16, 1918. Spike was an Irish actor, comedian, playwright, musician, and poet. He was born in Ahmednagar (Mumbai), India, and spent his early years there, after which he moved to the United Kingdom around 1931. Spike was not really a big fan of his first name and liked to be called "Spike", which he decided to do so, after hearing the band "Spike Jones and his city slickers". He was a prolific poet and writer. He wrote and edited many books, and some of his most famous works include Puckoon (1963). He not only wrote books but also wrote for a British radio programme "The

Goon Show". He was also the cast member and co-creator of this programme. The first series was set out from May 20 to September 20, 1951. He also wrote an autobiography of his time during World War 2 in the book "Adolf Hitler: My Part in His Downfall," released in 1971. Spike Milligan died at the age of 83 due to liver disease on February 27, 2002. He died peacefully at his home in Rye, East Sussex.

56th Heavy Regiment (1940)

"The Goon Show" was quite a popular show at that time, for which he is known. The programme had listeners in many different countries, including Australia, India, Canada, and New Zealand.

The show became very popular among people from different countries and helped him achieve international fame. The success of this show led him to create other television and radio comedy programs, some of which are "The Idiot Weekly" and "Fred". His international fame and status offered him many roles in films, and he successfully created comedy roles in them.

Many of the poems and stories he wrote were suitable for children. He wrote a few works, imitating some of the original works, like the Bible and Robin Hood. Most of his works were based on comedy and a sense of humour, but he also wrote a book on his memories of World War II.

Milligan was married to June Marlowe in 1952. In his marriage with June, they welcomed their three children, Laura, Sean, and Sile. June Marlowe was an American film actress and was known for her performance in "Our Gang Shorts" as "Miss Crabtree". Sadly, their marriage did not last long, and they ended their relationship in 1960. After breaking up with his first wife, in 1962, he married Patricia Ridgeway, also known as Paddy (who was also an actress). In his marriage with Patricia, they had one child, Jane Milligan, who was born in 1966. Unfortunately, they had a tragic separation. Their relationship ended in February 1978 when Patricia lost her life to breast cancer in

London, England. Spike Milligan was never a big fan of monogamy (being with a single person). Due to this fact, rumours were heard that he had many affairs with many women. Later, in 1975, he had an affair with Margaret Maughan, from whom he had a son in 1976. There is also another rumour that he had another daughter from his affair with a Canadian journalist, Robert Watt. In 1983, he got married to his third wife, Shelagh Sinclair. Sadly, their relationship ended with Spike Milligan's death in February 2002. After Spike Milligan's death, Shelagh did not marry anyone and died in June 2011.

Spike Milligan's 'will was left for his children, but after marrying Shelagh, his will was changed, leaving his entire real estate to Shelagh. The new will angered the children, and they tried to change the will, but with no luck. The will remain the same. Four of his children from the first two marriages collaborated with documentary makers and created a programme for Spike Milligan called "I Told You I Was Ill: The Life and Legacy of Spike Milligan" in 2005. Milligan suffered from bipolar disease and witnessed many serious mental breakdowns, most of which made him suffer for almost one year. He was brave enough to speak about his illness and how it affected his life in order to spread awareness among people. Milligan was born in India; his mother was British and his father was Irish. Spike Milligan served in the British Army for six years, and he felt he was entitled to British citizenship. He later spent most of his life in the United Kingdom, when British law gave him a secure place in the United Kingdom. In

1960, he applied for a British passport, but his application was rejected because he did not agree to the Oath of Allegiance. But later He became an Irish citizen in 1962 with the help of his Irish father, and later he achieved his rights as a British subject. Spike Milligan was raised as a Catholic and believed in Catholicism. Milligan was agnostic and believed there was a power that listened to us. In 1974, he was charged with shooting a trespasser with an air rifle, and later, when he was brought to court, he justified himself and was provided with a conditional discharge.

Milligan was not a really good student. He attended Paul's High School in Rangoon. His mother was British and his father was Irish, which gave him a place in the United Kingdom. He moved from India and relocated to London, where he spent most of his life. While he was in London, he attended Catford Boys School, St Saviours, and South East London Polytechnic in Lewisham. Spike Milligan had a net worth of $65 million. His primary career as a comedian has generated so much wealth for him. As per the record, the comedian had a luxurious lifestyle, along with all the facilities. Some of the records are not so clear and all of them are taken as an assumption, as the famous comedian lived and died years ago, and it is clearly very difficult to find the exact details of Milligan.

SPIKE MILLIGAN'S LIFE IN A NUTSHELL

Laughter and misery are often intertwined. SPIKE Milligan can be counted among the list. He was routinely hailed as a comedy genius. Spike Milligan is known for not being a good student due to his pranks. Before joining the British army, he worked as a jazz trumpeter in the late 1930s and early 1940s. He fought in the North Africa campaign and in the invasion of Italy. In the invasion, he was seriously injured and suffered shell shock, which is a type of post-traumatic stress disorder from a major explosion.

As we all know, Spike was an excellent writer. After he stopped serving in the British Army, he wrote a book on his experience during this time. "Hitler-My Part in His Downfall" was an honest and open account of his experience. But Spike did not back down from showing his dislike of authority and commanding officers. Spike suffered a long way with his injuries from the invasion. After recovering from the injuries, Spike actively got engaged in comic skits. In 1951 he made a partnership with Michael Bentine, Peter Sellers and Harry Secombe and created the program; The Goon Show". The programme helped the spread of post-war comedy. The show showed the struggle to find meaning in their lives and identity. The show became very popular among people for its wild sense of humour.

"The Goon Show" suddenly became a hit and gave Milligan international fame. As we all know, many famous people suffer from fame and pressure from the public. The same happened in Milligan's life. The fame and pressure had caused serious effects on his mental health. The show was such a great success that they had constant pressure to keep up the standard of the show. This caused serious damage to his mental health. The show went on for a while, and when it reached series three, Milligan underwent a serious mental breakdown and was hospitalised for two months for his recovery. Although the pressure gave him serious mental issues, it also gave him many chances to appear on film. In the late 60s and 70s, he got really involved in TV shows. He was seen in many comedy series and appeared in many guest roles. Spike had a great sense of humour. He was selected in the programme

"Bloom" to play the part of a serious character, but eventually, it turned out to be a comedy. At first, the cast was not very unhappy, but later went along with it. After some time, the programme was retitled "Son of Bloom" and was moved to comedy theatre. Milligan was well-known for his poetry, with the majority of his works aimed at children. Milligan also gave his contributions to cartoons to the satirical magazine Private Eye, most of which were only one-line jokes.

THE GOON SHOW

Milligan joined with Peter Sellers, Harry Secombe and Michael Bentine and created a comedy programme "The Goon Show". At first, the BBC gave the show the title "Crazy People". The show helped to spread post-war comedy among people.

The show suddenly became a hit and gave Milligan international fame. This helped him gain the attention of directors and he got many offers for films. The show portrayed characters having imaginary friends. The programme showcased characters struggling to find meaning in life and escape their identities.

The first episode of the show aired on BBC Home Service on May 28, 1951. In the beginning, Milligan did not showcase much in the program, but later, as the show went by, he made quite an impressive effort and became the lead. He played a wide range of characters, including Minnie Bannister, Eccles, Count Moriarty, and Jim Spriggs. He wrote many scripts and co-wrote many scripts with many collaborators.

Some of his most notable collaborators who worked with him were Larry Stephens (radio scriptwriter) and Eric Sykes (English TV writer for radio and television).

In the early days, he wrote most of his work collaborating with Stephens, and the work was edited by Jimmy Grafton, but their partnership ended when it reached series 3. Series 3 was really tough for Milligan.

As we know, many famous actors suffer from the pressure of fame. In like manner, Milligan was also affected by the fame and pressure of the show. By the time it reached series 3, Milligan had a mental breakdown and was hospitalised for two months for his recovery. Series 4 was mostly written by Milligan, but by the time it reached series 5, he could not contribute much due to the birth of his second child, Sean.

In series 6, he collaborated with Eric Sykes, who is a stage, radio, television, and film writer. Milligan later got back with Stephens in Series 6, but unfortunately, that did not last as Stephens had met with health issues and Milligan collaborated with John Antrobus, who is an English playwright and screenwriter. Milligan's and Stephens's partnership ended tragically in 1959 when Stephens died due to a brain haemorrhage.

The first year of the show was recorded live, but by series 4, they had the idea of adopting the idea of using magnetic tape. Spike Milligan put forth the idea of editing the tapes and creating ground-breaking sound effects. The BBC engineers' limits were pushed to their limits by Mulligan's complex sound effects. With the help of the magnetic tape, the sounds could be produced in advance.

The writing and pressure in "The Goon Show" caused his mental illness and killed his first marriage. Another achievement in his life as a writer was his involvement in the Associated London Scripts agency.

During this time, he got married to his first wife, June Marlowe, and he could not focus much on writing, which led him to accept the invitation from Eric Sykes, with whom he collaborated on "The Goon Show," which eventually led to the creation of the cooperative agency.

SPIKE MILLIGAN'S RISE TO HIS FAME: THE WRITING SIDE

Spike Milligan is known for his humorous writing, and several of his works have won awards for best comedic poem in the UK. To express his thoughts concerning every aspect of his life, including the family to losing loved ones in the war to other matters that were important to him, Spike also produced a corpus of serious poetry. Milligan had a great sense of humour and wished to become an entertainer, but sadly, life does not give you everything you want. He was nearly as well-known for his battles with manic depression and his outbursts against human foolishness, especially the British type, as he was for his subtle humour that made him a British icon and influenced following generations of British entertainers.

Even though he was really passionate about comedy, his first was in a nuts-and-bolts factory in London. He never gave up the ambition of becoming an entertainer. He learned to play many musical instruments, including guitar, ukulele, and trumpet, and really showed a keen interest in jazz music. He won the Bing Crosby singing competition held at the Lewish Hippodrome. Milligan served six years in the British army and was listed for many military services. He met Harry Secombe while he was serving in the British army in North Africa. He later collaborated with Harry in "The Goon Show". It was really difficult for him to get into the industry. His friend from the army, Harry Secombe, helped him and introduced him to Peter Sellers and Michael Bentine. The team used to hang out in Jimmy Grafton's Pub. The four of them had an enormous sense of humour and created bits of comedy in the back room of the pub.

56th Heavy Regiment (Italy, 23 December 1943)

Jimmy Grafton was a producer, writer, and theatrical agent who also served in World

War II. Grafton himself was a writer and a radio comedian. He collaborated with Milligan and they became co-writers. Grafton wrote gags for Derek Roy, and when he collaborated with Milligan, he also wrote gags for them.

He had shown a keen interest in music and comedy, so he used his inherent talent and worked as a musician during the late 1930s and the beginning of the 1940s. He served in the British army and fought in the war with Nazi Germany. He performed comedy while he served in the army. He used to entertain his co-soldiers with his comedy and played the guitar for a comedy group called "The Bill Hall Trio". Milligan performed as a jazz vocalist, guitarist, and trumpeter. During the Second World War, he contributed-used his service as a radioman in a D battery. Milligan used to perform during the Second World War, and he had the finest pitch. During wartime, he had experience using rifles. This was clearly mentioned in part two of Adolf Hitler's memoirs. He was also appointed as a lance bombardier during the battle of Monte Cassino. During this battle, he was wounded in action. Later, he was hospitalised, and his major wound was in his right leg. Another incident that was mentioned was when Jenkins invited Gunners Milligan and Edgington to his campsite to play jazz with him. Only to showcase to him that gunners were far superior to the ability to play "Whistling Rufus". After he got hospitalized, Milligan had several military jobs, and due to his injury later, he became a full-time entertainer. He used multiple instruments like jazz and guitar and also was engaged in a comedy group named The Bill Hall Trio. The troop attended concert parties for the betterment of the troops. After getting retired from the military, he remained plain in Italy and later returned to Britain. After reaching Britain he started writing parodies, which eventually led to "The Goon Show".

He became really famous for his radio programme "The Goon Show," which gave him fame and many opportunities. After the success of this show, many television shows, plays, and films imitated the play. He was also famous for the television series he created for children in 1995, "Wolves, Witches and Giants" It was an adaptation of classic fairy tales which featured wolves, witches, and giants. He started his entertaining career with the creation of "The Goon Show." After "The Goon Show," he got engaged in his work "Treasure Ireland." The play was exhibited at the Mermaid Theatre in London. The play was a huge success, which motivated him to go for his next project, which was The Bed Sitting Room. The play was co-written with John Antrobus and was exhibited at three theatres; the Mermaid Theatre, the Duke of York's Theatre, and the Comedy Theatre in the year 1963. The bed sitting room was so popular that later it was turned into a film. After this, his next project was Oblomove, which was staged at the Lyric Theatre, Hammersmith, in the year 1964. He appeared in Q5 and The World of the Beachcomber, which were aired on British television. He was often seen on television and radio after the great success of his first programme the Goon Show". He appeared in many films, including The Three Musketeers in 1973, The Last Remark on the Ark of Beau Geste in 1977, and Monty Python's Life of Brain in 1978. He also toured internationally with his comedy routine.

It's important to approach Spike Milligan's poems with a sense of humour. One would be quite let down if they attempted to analyse his works from a rigorous analytical standpoint. Especially in the way the poem is recited, the material is purely for fun. There are perhaps works like There are Holes in the Sky where one might discover some of the wonder and logic of childhood, but this would be straining the goal a bit. A hazy attempt to address the why, what, and how questions is one subject that runs across the poetry. The Lion's absurd lines serve as confirmation of this. The reader is presented with a circumstance right away that most people would not experience. Further, it is explained to the reader that when being assaulted, she or he ought to do a few specific actions. There is minimal credit given to the response where this tackles the hypothetical "what if" inquiry that a kid could ask. Most definitely, this is the poem's main goal.

The poetry fits the definition of poetry even if it is meant to make people smile and laugh. It's amazing that Spike Milligan's writing has continued to be widely read despite the fact that many literary critics have dismissed it. One of the top 10 rhymes recited by toddlers in the UK is his most well-known poetry, On the Ning Nang Nong. Also in 1998, one of his poems, "On the Nang Nong" was selected as the UK's favourite comic poem. Readers of all of Spike Milligan's writings will notice that not everything in his writing is silly and amusing. Although the majority of the work is light hearted readers must realise that Spike Milligan, like many others who went through similar periods as he did, experienced mental health issues following the First and Second World Wars. Others have noted the depressive episodes and nervous breakdowns he had. Instead of letting his actions speak for themselves, let's concentrate on the qualities for which he is well-known.

Milligan started his acting career in the Mermaid Theatre by playing the character "Ben Gunn". Treasure Island was played daily twice from 1961-1962. Later, it became an annual production at the Mermaid Theatre. In the play, Spike played the character Ben Gunn; Barry Humphries, who is an Australian actor, comedian, author, and great satirist, played the role of Long John Silver; and William Rushton, who is an English cartoonist, satirist, and actor, played the character Squire Trelawney. Milligan showed extraordinary performance in that and surely the best role of his was "Ben Gunn". He was the heart of the show and stole people's hearts. He almost spent one hour in the make-up room before he went on stage. The children loved him, and were very much delighted to see him on stage. Milligan and John Antrobus, an English screenwriter and playwright, planned on exploring the dramatized post-nuclear world and shared this idea with Miles. The show

"The Bedsitting Room" was aired on Marlowe Theatre on February 12, 1962. The show was written in collaboration with Spike Milligan and John Antrobus. It was a huge success and also appeared at the Saville Theatre in 1967 in London. The show was later adapted into films due to its star's fame and success. The script of Oblomov by Aragno was later bought in 1964 by Milligan's production company. Milligan worked hard for this novel; he had high hopes for turning it from comedy to serious. The novel was performed as an improv comedy, an art form where improvisers work without any script. It soon became a hit, breaking all the other records. It was later renamed to "Son of Oblomov" and officially moved to a comedy theatre.

His writings were mostly filled with comedy. Spike Milligan shares the experiences he had during the time of Hitler and the Second World War in the book, Adolf Hitler: My Role in His Destruction. The book was published in the year 1971 by Michael Joseph. It published the first volume of his war memories. Milligan published seven volumes of his war memories. In his books, Milligan shares his struggles and mental breakdowns. Milligan was never afraid to show his dislike for the officials. He represented the stories through some rough sketches of narrative ante cedes and comic sketches. The book was later turned into a film with the same title.

BEHIND THE LAUGHTER

Comedy artists can elicit laughter because they frequently exhibit traits associated with schizophrenia or bipolar disorder. According to studies that seem to corroborate the commonly held view that there is a relationship between lunacy and creativity, their knack for amusing people resides in having odd personalities and showing what experts claim are high degrees of psychotic features. Spike Milligan, who endured a lifetime of manic depression. He "created the wacky humour and the wildly absurd concepts that were the hallmark of his despair by using the freely associating mental processes of his manic periods."

Stephen Fry has made significant contributions to bringing attention to depression as a medical condition. Spike Milligan suffered from severe depression for the majority of his life. Additionally, Spike Milligan was praised for working to save not only the world's threatened fauna, but also the neighbourhood's trees. He frequently succeeded in his attempts to draw others into some plan or initiative. This is more about a broad, all-encompassing endeavour, typically with a societal benefit as its objective, than it is about a private business or lonely hobby. There is a goal in sight, however narcissistic the person's behaviour may appear to be.

He put in more effort than nearly any other entertainer that comes to mind, yet his copious production sometimes seemed to lack a clear sense of what was worthwhile and what was hasty self-indulgence. He appeared to become more relaxed in his final years, but there was always a glimmer of the perilous flame that had repeatedly driven him to the verge of hopelessness and ignited laughter to purge us all. Both Milligan and Sellers had instances of physical aggression, but Sellers deliberately avoided receiving mental care, in contrast to Milligan's many hospitalizations. In addition to accepting electroshock therapy, Milligan also sought advice from Sydney Gottlieb, a psychiatrist who saw patients at the Ronnie Scott's Jazz Club, where he played trumpet. Danger, dread, brutality, and murder just weren't far away for Milligan and his Goons. But other than when he was experiencing an emotional breakdown, Milligan usually used his aggression for good.

He had frequent depression episodes and held on for dear life. He was on the verge of giving up during one of his darkest episodes around late 1990 and late 1991. He became so depressed and treatment-resistant that ECT, a last resort for a small percentage of patients, was even administered to him. Then, a month prior to Christmas in 1991, his sadness abruptly subsided. He was praised for persevering. He reverted to his former creative, witty, gregarious, and energetic self.

SPIKE MILLIGAN'S LEGACY

A regular correspondent to Graves since the 1960s, Milligan usually addressed questions regarding classical studies in his letters. The letters are part of Graves's bequest to St. John's College. After Milligan's death, Sean Hughes starred in the film Puckoon, which also featured his daughter, actress Jane Milligan. He lived in Holden Road, Woodside Park, Finchley, and The Crescent, Barnet, and was a major contributor to the Finchley Society. The old house in Woodside Park has been demolished, but a blue plaque honours him on the block of apartments there. In his former home of Finchley, a bronze bench features a likeness of Milligan. For ten years, Barbara Warren led the Finchley Society to raise funds to commission a monument to Milligan by sculptor John Somerville, which was erected on Avenue House's grounds on East End Road. Showbusiness celebrities and Local dignitaries attended the unveiling ceremony on September 4, 2014, which included Maureen Lipman, Roy Hudd, Terry Gilliam, Michael Parkinson, Kathy Lette, Lynsey de Paul, and Denis Norden.

His childhood home in the London Borough of Lewisham has been the subject of a campaign for a statue. In the 1930s, he moved to the UK from India, lived at 50 Riseldine Road, Brockley, and attended Brownhill Boys' School. An area in the Wadestown Library, Wellington, New Zealand, called Spike Milligan Corner, has a plaque and bench dedicated to him. He was named the

"Comedians' Comedian" in a 2005 poll, where fellow comedians and comedy insiders voted him among the top 50 comedy acts. The Spike Milligan memorial bench in the garden of Stephen's House in Finchley is where he was voted the "funniest person of the last 1,000 years" in a BBC poll in August 1999. As a child, Milligan played his father in the movie Adolf Hitler: My Part in His Downfall, with Jim Dale portraying him. A second film adaptation of his novel was The Life and Death of Peter Sellers (2003), in which Edward Tudor-Pole portrayed Milligan as his father. Michael Barrymore portrayed Milligan in Surviving Spike; a stage plays from 2008. On June 9, 2006, it was revealed that Richard Wiseman had named Milligan as the author of the joke that the Laugh lab project had deemed to be the funniest in the entire globe. According to Wiseman, the joke included each of the three components of a good gag: anxiety, a sense of superiority, and a sense of surprise.

Milligan was referred to as "The Godfather of Alternative Comedy" by Eddie Izzard. Ideas that had no limitations arose from his free mind. Additionally, he had an impact on a new generation of comedians who became known as "alternative." He was well-regarded by Monty Python cast members. In a widely circulated interview at the time, John Cleese said that "Milligan is the Great God to all of us." When Milligan was vacationing in Tunisia, close to where the movie was being made, and he was returning to the place where he had been stationed during the war, the Pythons granted him a cameo role in their

1979 film, Monty Python's Life of Brian. He was given a small role in yellow beard by Graham Chapman. After they retired, Desmond, Milligan's younger brother, and his parents all migrated to Australia. His mother spent the remainder of her long life on the Central Coast of New South Wales, just north of Sydney, in the coastal community of Woy Woy. He began to frequently travel to Australia as a result, where he produced a variety of radio and television shows, including The Idiot Weekly with Bobby Limb. While visiting his mother in Woy Woy, he also penned a number of books, including Puckoon. When visiting the town in the 1960s, Milligan referred to it as "the largest above-ground cemetery in the world." As a form of protest against the circumstances that prevented her son from obtaining British citizenship, Milligan's mother became an Australian citizen in 1985. At the same time, Milligan was rumoured to be considering applying for Australian citizenship. In honour of him, the Woy Woy Public Library's conference room and the suspension bridge connecting Woy Woy and Gosford were dubbed the Spike Milligan Bridge.

NOTABLE AWARDS OF SPIKE MILLIGAN

An honorary knighthood was introduced in 2000 to a slew of honours. It was honorary since his father's Irish ancestry prevented him from automatically obtaining British citizenship and the formal title, which had earlier caused a great deal of controversy. He has received various awards and has been nominated for various categories too; they are the following during his career. He received the BAFTA TV Award in 1957 for the Best Writer category. He received the award for best comedian at the British Comedy Awards. He got a Lifetime Achievement Award in 1994 for his long and successful career from the early 40s to the late 90s. The Hugo Awards for Best Dramatic Presentation were won for the play, "The Bed

Sitting Room," in 1969. Even though he was an Irish writer, he received most of the awards for his contributions to British comedies.

SPIKE MILLIGAN'S DEATH

Even at his last stage, Milligan did not seem to lose his sense of dark humour. He commented on his war friend Harry Secombe's (who was really close to Milligan) death by saying "I am Glad he died before me because I did not want him to sing at my funeral". Harry was Milligan's close friend from the army and later he collaborated with him in his show "The Goon Show". A song that was sung by Harry was played at Milligan's memorial service. Spike Milligan wrote his own obituary, in which he stated repeatedly that he created the Goon Show. The Goon Show was a great performance and no one dared to question its success. Milligan suffered from bipolar disease due to the fame and pressure. He was diagnosed with the disease. Milligan died at the age of 83 due to kidney failure in his home in Rye. His coffin was carried to St. Thomas Church. As a symbol of respect and love, his coffin was covered with the flag of Ireland. Milligan wished to have the words "I told you I was ill" in his epitaph, but the church refused to have that. And later, they came to a compromise and wrote in Gaelic. It is said that his headstone was removed from the church and moved near to his wife, and later it was returned to its original location.

CONCLUSION

In top to his role as comedian, Spike was also an actor, poet, and writer. He was a multifaceted figure who wrote numerous books, produced countless radio and television comedies, and appeared in a number of movies. Despite the fact that he produced many excellent pieces of art, "The Goon Show," a radio comedy series, served as his passport to fame and is still known for. The show's nine-year popularity was attributed to Milligan, who the audience enthusiastically embraced as a damaged but lovable genius. He then established himself as a well-known voice on radio and television and published a number of oddly amusing autobiographical and other books, as well as comedic poems, much of it intended for young readers. In addition, he is an absurdist and nonsensical humourist. Spike was eager to take a stand on important matters. He was a vocal supporter of environmental protection and animal rights. Spike would speak up on any matter, no matter how trivial. In addition to being humorously inspired, Milligan was also capable of being passionate, compassionate, and kind. His life is a mixture of both light and darkness, from his early years in India through his early career as a jazz musician and sketch-show entertainer, his time serving with the Royal Artillery in North Africa and Italy, to that fateful first broadcast of The Goon Show and beyond into the pages of history of comedy history. The show's nine-year popularity was attributed to Milligan, who the audience enthusiastically embraced as a damaged but lovable genius. In addition to being humorously inspired, Milligan was also capable of being passionate, compassionate, and kind. Being devoted to them, he would spend hours playing games with them, such as composing fairy messages that he then concealed beneath stones in the yard for them to discover. A few of Spike's tolerant creative collaborators saw the manic side of him. Neil Shand, a co-writer on Q5, explained to Carpenter how the former Goon would vomit funny ideas at an uncontrollable rate before slowing down in melancholy, sadness, and tiredness. Traditional depression. But tragic genius Spike Milligan completely revolutionised English humour with his life.

Extras

A Humble Request

Our books are intended to indulge you. If you enjoyed this book or gained any valuable information from it in any way, feel free to share your experience with us. Your contented reviews will help to boost us not only in the sales perspective but also to improve our creativity. Please leave a review at the store front where you purchased this book, and it would be greatly appreciated.

Related Books

Viola Davis' Days - From Poverty to Oscar: Life and Achievements Of The Actress Viola Davis, The First African-American To Achieve The Triple Crown Of Acting

The enchanting journey of Actress Viola Davis from the grip of poverty to the pinnacle of acting success is now at your fingertips. Click to unlock.

US : https://amzn.to/3SrRc4Z

UK : https://amzn.to/3ClX8XB

Dave Grohl, Melodic Nirvana of a Foo Fighter: Abridged Life Story of an American Music Legend, Dave Grohl

Feel the vibes of Dave Grohl who makes hex on instruments with bands and friends. Click for an exclusive experience.

US : https://amzn.to/3UOjF6B

UK : https://amzn.to/3fp2Sqt

Big Yin - Billy Connolly: Tale of Billy Connolly and the Way He Nourished His Willpower from Morbidity

Attain this book to know the tale of the survival of comic Big Yin, who bravely fought in front of all which was sentenced that there's no cure.

US : https://amzn.to/3fk4iT9

UK : https://amzn.to/3E6ZLoO

Can't Just Chuckle – The Richard Osman Book: Unofficial Guide to the monumental moments of The English comedian Richard Osman's Life, In Short

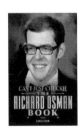

This quietly moving book is the quick read on the towering Richard Osman, the Pointless guy whose debut book is breaking all records. Get a copy!

US : https://amzn.to/3SprEWf

UK : https://amzn.to/3T1MwD1

Matthew McConaughey, Undazed and Unconfused: All rights about Matthew McConaughey

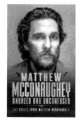

To know all about the quintessential Texan Mathew McConaughey, his quest to find the meaning of life, how he engineered his destiny-Buy the book.

US : https://amzn.to/3fz0Y73

UK : https://amzn.to/3SscMXd

I am Seth, Seth Rogen: The Life & Ventures of Seth Aaron Rogen

A book to make you laugh and think, a book to celebrate levity, grab a copy soon to know more about the man who made you laugh like a maniac!

US : https://amzn.to/3dRSCGW

UK : https://amzn.to/3SLBTDU

Sinéad O'Connor, The Unofficial Biography: Sinead O'Connor's Life Story In Short

Sinead O'Connor stole Prince's song, became a star; and then destroyed her career. Buy a copy now to read the story of the most controversial pop star.

US : https://amzn.to/3rlW93A

UK : https://amzn.to/3y0D4re

Andrew McCarthy, Dwelling Down Into 80's Brat Pack Era: A Nostalgic Memoir

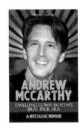

Hunting high and low for a nostalgia-inducing book to immerse yourself in the 80s world? Get the book to know about Andrew McCarthy, the Brat Packer.

US : https://amzn.to/3BOlLLa

UK : https://amzn.to/3BTW9wl

Being Billie: Billie Eilish, A Short Life Story

Dark, but poignantly so, like Billie Eilish's songs, this book brings you her life's trials and triumphs in a candid narration. Buy a copy now!

US : https://amzn.to/3fk6dHl

UK : https://amzn.to/3dRJEte

Will Power Smith: Will Smith's Way to Success

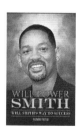

Grab your copy to be inspired by the life of Will Smith, who came from rap-acting, faced strains & won success, beaten his sad infancy & other chains.

US : https://amzn.to/3Ssi19l

UK : https://amzn.to/3BYZfiP

Arnold's Iron Mind: Learn & Inherit Arnold Schwarzenegger's Dream Achieving Mindset, Strategies and Techniques Which Made Him Mr. Olympia, Film Star and Governor of California

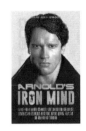

What if I say that you could inherit the success system and mindset of Arnold Schwarzenegger, which made his dreams come true thrice? Click & have it.

US : https://amzn.to/3dS5qxc

UK : https://amzn.to/3SMDObg

A Woman Called Cicely Tyson: The Remarkable Life of an Iconic African-American Women

This book deals with the amazingly talented African- American actress Cecily Tyson who broke the prejudice of the Hollywood industry.

US : https://amzn.to/3E5lUvt

UK : https://amzn.to/3dS7Hsb

Many Days of Daisy May: Daisy May Cooper's Incredible Life Moments Depicted In Short

US : https://amzn.to/3y5fUjA

UK : https://amzn.to/3CnM2Sa

Jennifer Grey, Dancing Out Of The Corner: The Acclaimed Actress Jennifer Grey's Abridged Biography

You wanna know how Jennifer Grey crossed hellish thorny paths on her ride to success, depending heavily on her mental strength? Come, click and read.

US : https://amzn.to/3Stt4is

UK : https://amzn.to/3CmFm6C

Keanu Reeves, The Story: The Way Keanu Reeves Become Himself [Unofficial]

Get your copy right away to know the dark pages of the life of Keanu Reeves, who overcame the pains from a row of problems and shines in the films.

US : https://amzn.to/3SsdDqG

UK : https://amzn.to/3dP9MoR

Miriam Being A Maverick: Unconventional Ways of The Actress Miriam Margolyes

You are just a click away to unravel the unusual life and acts of the anomalous actress Miriam Margolyes. Click, read and have a whale of a time.

US : https://amzn.to/3E1Tu6F

UK : https://amzn.to/3y3FCFa

The Fights Sheila Fought: Sheila Hancock Fast Read Bio Book

Do you know how Sheila Hancock endured through times of severe pain and loss, and still stands high at 89? Click to reveal her spirited tenacity.

US : https://amzn.to/3E5LiSX

UK : https://amzn.to/3fvwlPR

This is Tunde Oyeneyin: A Sprint Through Her Life and Strategies

Tunde Oyeneyin's tale that guides to fitness, Tips and tricks for fitness from the most inspiring Peloton instructor.

US : https://amzn.to/3E3N1be

UK : https://amzn.to/3y39AZM

Molly-Mae, A Fast Read Bio: Life of a social media influencer

Molly is a genius, who at a young age, fell prey to setbacks. Pick this to explore her life of tasting success by holding the hands of her suitor.

US : https://amzn.to/3REFPWp

UK : https://amzn.to/3LRXjxb

The Times of Melvyn Bragg: Bio, Unofficial & Crisp, Made For Fast Read

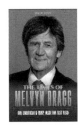

Bragg's a prodigy born amid the tumult of WW2 & has a very emotional bond with his mother. Grab to know some chapters of that life mixed with pain.

US : https://amzn.to/3fApOn2

UK : https://amzn.to/3rgTPuD

THE END

Printed in Great Britain
by Amazon